In 1850, a father and son escape from the cruelty of slavery on a southern plantation with the help from abolitionists. But how could they soul-travel The Underground Railroad into our modern world today?

This thought provoking book explores historical and startling realities which can explain many inexplicable coincidences and happenings in our lives as well as the concept of reincarnation.

THE
BEFORE *Love*

A fugitive slave father and son soul-travel
The Underground Railroad into today

LINDA THORN

Balboa Press books may be ordered through booksellers or by contacting:

Balboa Press
A Division of Hay House
1663 Liberty Drive
Bloomington, IN 47403
www.balboapress.com
1 (877) 407-4847

ISBN: 978-1-9822-2067-9 (sc)
ISBN: 978-1-9822-2068-6 (e)

Print information available on the last page.

Balboa Press rev. date: 03/21/2019

BALBOA.
PRESS
A DIVISION OF HAY HOUSE

Contents

Dedicated to My Aunt Dorothy

A few years ago, I was struggling with a life-changing decision and was fortunate to receive a *visit* from my aunt Dorothy who had died twenty years before. I was amazed and thrilled to see her so vibrant, healthy and seemingly alive because the last time I saw her, she was near death in the hospital and her earthly body was emaciated by cancer. In this visit from beyond, she gave me advice which turned my life in a wonderful direction. I never *saw* my aunt Dorothy again. But I feel that she is always near and I am so grateful for this spiritual connection and phenomenal experience.

Author's Preface

Over hundreds of years of slavery in the United States, there were as few as 100,000 who escaped from the estimated 4 million southern slaves in total. The period of time referred to as The Underground Railroad in this book specifically covers the period after 1850.

In 1834, slavery was abolished in Britain and all of its many colonies around the world, including Canada, known at the time as British North America and much smaller than Canada is today.

Prior to 1850, slave owners in the American slave States could recapture escaped slaves. Runaway slaves who reached American non slave, northern States were considered 'free'. But in 1850, the United States government passed The Fugitive Slave Act. This meant that any black could be captured by bounty hunters and taken as a slave to a southern plantation. So every escaped slave and even 'free' blacks and their children born in non-slave States were subject to this new law. There was then a surge of about 40,000 slaves on southern plantations and other free northern blacks who escaped on The Underground Railroad to freedom in Canada. In 1865 at the end of The Civil War slavery was abolished in the United States.

Canada was referred to as *Glory Land* and *Freedom Land* in many gospel songs sung by slaves labouring in the southern fields. These key words were secret codes for escape. It was known that once you crossed the border, bridges and rivers or lakes into Canada with the help of abolitionists on The Underground Railroad, slaves became *free* people who were safe from previous owners or bounty hunters. This is a story of two slaves who escaped in the past and were re-united in today's world… in another lifetime.

Lisa was a lovely little girl who was adopted from across the sea.
She now had a forever home in a big, busy city with her new family.

Her new mom and dad were thrilled to hug and kiss
Their beautiful addition to the family as was their wish.

Lisa's dad was a psychiatrist who helped people talk about things.
Her mom was a librarian who loved books
about history with queens and kings.

Mom was so happy that she would talk to no end
On her cell phone to Opreena, her very best friend.

Oh, all the clever things that little Lisa could do
Like sing and draw and tie her new pink shoes.

Opreena was delighted to be told that her birthday now was shared
With little Lisa, so it seemed they were coincidentally paired.

The day came when finally they would meet.
Auntie Opreena brought a welcome gift for such a celebration treat.

When Auntie "O" first saw happy Lisa's big eyes,
She got an enormous surprise!

Lisa joyously shouted "KINTU" out loud
To everyone's amazement in the crowd.

Lisa kissed and hugged Auntie "O" and couldn't let her go.
Mom and dad were pleased, but wanted to know

How Lisa seemed to recognize Auntie and called her by a strange name.
Soon their lives would never be the same.

With each new day, Lisa sang and made up songs
But her parents began to worry that something might be wrong.

Lisa often whispered to her doll, "Shh, do not talk."
As she gently led her doll in a single file walk.

She seemed to help both of them into a small rowboat
And across the border river by moonlight they would pretend to float.

Lisa crooned to her doll that they would soon be safe at last.
In a place they called 'Freedom Land' from the distant past.

Lisa's parents were accepting but curious to understand
How Lisa seemed to know Auntie "O" from a faraway land.

One day Auntie "O" saw Lisa playing with her
doll this way and her heart felt whole
Because she knew that the same feeling was deep in her own soul.

Auntie "O" had a dream that night
And eventually everything seemed so right.

Auntie dreamed that long ago she was a southern, black slave boy
Who brought his slave father so much love and joy.

Lisa's new mom did some computer research to discover facts from clues
And the story pieced together made some important news.

Canada was the most northerly stop on the secret
Underground Railroad for fugitive slave emancipation.

Before 1865, many compassionate people helped slaves escape
across the border and waterways to this free nation.

At work, Lisa's dad helped Auntie to talk more about her dream state
And Auntie "O" finally discovered their past fate…

Lisa was the slave father in a past life.
The new mom and dad used to be the helpful Quaker man and wife.

Auntie "O" was the slave boy who was softly shushed to be quiet and hide
Until kind Quaker Abolitionists led them safely to the other shore's side.

By watching little Lisa at play today,
Could this really have happened that way?

When Lisa was gently asked why she sang
those gospel 'Glory Land' songs,
She quietly answered that the slaves sang those
to pray for a free land 'to belong'.

Auntie "O" and Lisa experienced a very strong connection
That was based on past love and real affection,

When in another life, one was a slave father, one was his son…
That is really when the BEFORE LOVE had begun.

Reincarnation

HOW LONG HAS REINCARNATION BEEN KNOWN?

The belief in reincarnation has been accepted by Hindus, Buddhists and some other Eastern Religions for thousands of years. It was referenced in the Old and New Testaments of the early Bible and Gnostics (Greek: *gnosis* or knowledge) of that era believed in reincarnation. In 553 A.D., emperor Justinian presided over a council of church bishops which declared that belief in reincarnation was a heresy.

WHAT IS REINCARNATION?

Reincarnation is the concept that each body has a soul within from a *Divine Source* or *Intelligent, Loving Force* and by free will that same soul is born into a chosen body each of many lifetimes. In reincarnation, the belief is that there is no death, just energy transformations from temporary human lives on earth returning always to *the other side* where souls are at *home*. "Just when the caterpillar thought the world was over, she became a butterfly."- Barbara Haines Howett.

WHY DO SOULS REINCARNATE?

For a soul to gain spiritual growth, the soul requires a chosen human experience. The *quest* of the soul is to over many, many lifetimes, learn lessons and reach levels of higher consciousness towards spiritual enlightenment and a universal collective consciousness. Souls endeavour to overcome through their life experiences, feelings of greed, jealousy, grief, fear, hate, egotism, cruelty, selfishness, meanness, irresponsibility and inhumanity towards other sentient beings, etc. The *purpose* is to gain spiritual understanding and express higher vibrations of love and compassion for a better world of equality and peace. Showing compassion, grace and having an attitude of gratitude is part of the goal. It is not what our experiences are but how we react to them that show our soul success. Think of our earth as being a cosmic school where we need to pass these courses in order to graduate as a better human and advanced soul.

Albert Einstein said that 'earth is the insane asylum of the universe'. This planet is where we have profound experiences. After many lifetimes of gaining and attaining spiritual enlightenment, we may choose not to reincarnate anymore and can remain at *home* to help other souls.

HOW CAN THE BELIEF IN REINCARNATION HELP HUMANS?

There would be no racism if everyone realized that we reincarnate throughout the ages as different genders, skin colors, capabilities, personalities, talents, shapes and sizes, nationalities, and religions for the experiences. For example, expressing harsh judgment or hatred towards another group of people, may mean that your soul will choose to reincarnate into that group next lifetime to experience the hatred. Eventually we ought to become more tolerant and compassionate through many lifetimes. There would be no slavery or wars on earth if all souls learned that *Love is Everything*. A certified past-life regressionist can connect you with pertinent past lives that will help you improve understanding of your current life. But anyone can learn meditation techniques to travel within your soul to seek wisdom from past lives.

You can be spiritual without belonging to any particular religion or any religion at all though many religions include reincarnation as a fundamental belief. Believing in reincarnation fulfills a need for peace and healing on the planet. We all experience suffering on earth but our mission is to experience bliss and harmony as well. Share your joy. Try to make someone smile every day, can be a basic goal. Your inner journey allows you to seek higher truths and find balance of body, mind and soul energies to become your authentic self.

WHEN DO SOULS REINCARNATE?

Souls have free will and choose when to reincarnate into a specific body at birth because there are lessons to learn and specific experiences to have in each reincarnated life. The soul maintains all of their *spirit world* knowledge in the subconscious but at each birth, a *veil of forgetfulness* helps to begin a new life ready for new lessons on earth.

Talents from a former life may explain the incredulous composing abilities of a child prodigy named Wolfgang Amadeus Mozart who was proficient on keyboard and violin by the age of five years old in the classical era of music. Some souls bring beauty and music to the world and his long lasting musical legacy is still a phenomenon.

DO YOU REINCARNATE ALONE?

No. Soul friends reincarnate with us in each lifetime to accompany and help us on our journey. Each time, they take on roles as different family members, friends, partners and work mates in every one of your reincarnated lives. Have you experienced déjà vu? It is a feeling of something or someone new being so familiar. It can be a location that you *know* very well even though you have never been there in this lifetime. Often it is a feeling of complete knowing and implicit trust in a new acquaintance. You feel like you've known this person forever… these people are soul mates or otherworldly friends who you are very familiar with on *the other side*. Experiencing a very *bad gut feeling* about another person can be someone who you've had a negative experience with in a past lifetime and you may have lessons to learn from each other in this lifetime. Sometimes it is a sad life lesson but necessary for personal growth.

AM I EVER REALLY ALONE ON EARTH?

No. You may fear at times, that you are physically or emotionally alone. But trust that you have invisible Spirit Guides always near you. Never lose confidence in yourself and know that you are loved here and from beyond. Pay attention to coincidences as they can be a *nudge* or a *smile* from the spirit world to remind you that every life is connected and meaningful and that you are on the right track.

HOW CAN MY LIFE LESSONS HELP ME PROGRESS?

Every experience in life is an opportunity to learn, overcome and progress. Technology is advancing more every day. For example, imagine you are experiencing cyber-bullying. Our computer technology has so much potential to better humanity but there are certain mean and negative people who take advantage of this technology to experience power over others. They can cowardly disrupt the lives of others with lies or bullying on social media. Never let any other body on earth bully you into diminished self-worth in on-line cyberspace. Do not give your power to another. You are too precious to the world. Just use your *spiritual cell phone* to connect for advice within. Then use your *real cell phone* to tell your parents, another loved one, favourite teacher, a trusted friend or mentor. Take the situation from the dark of the coward to your evolving light. This is a life lesson you want to learn and succeed at rather than not which can cause harm and heartbreak.

HOW CAN I CONNECT WITH SPIRIT WORLD?

Spirituality is a personal journey within yourself, seeking to discover the reason of one's existence. It is your inner soul work. Ironically, you need to go *within* to reach *outward* to the universal collective consciousness. Since 1920, there has been the Self-Realization Fellowship in Los Angeles, California and many more centres around the world. Buddhist Centres and Hindu Temples can be found all over the world, including the United States and Canada. You can learn to be individually mindful and practice meditation for spiritual guidance and learning about chakras using CDs, DVDs, on-line instructions, chanting, certified mentors and specific yoga classes. This calming meditation experience is like a quiet prayer time. Don't be discouraged, it takes time to calm our busy minds and relax into mindfulness to seek and connect with a higher collective consciousness. In The Chronicles of Narnia books, author C.S. Lewis writes of the Great Lion, Aslan who appears like a loving, all knowing Divine Being with mystical powers who offers guidance and lessons to be learned at a higher level of consciousness. "You would not have called to me unless I had been calling to you." – Aslan, in the book, The Silver Chair.

Spiritualism involves other special humans who have been gifted with paranormal energies and abilities to help you communicate with spirits beyond the grave and others who offer psychic advice. One of the largest spiritual centres since 1879 is in Lily Dale, New York State. There are many world renowned individuals with specific metaphysical talents there and the purpose of the centre is to further science and philosophy in spiritualism. In 1931, Edgar Cayce and his supporters founded the Association for Research and Enlightenment (A.R.E.) in Virginia Beach, Virginia with centres throughout the world…'Each soul has a unique purpose and reason for being on this earth'.

Science and Spirituality connections are gaining interest in several organizations. *The Institute of Noetic Sciences* was co-founded in 1973 by Apollo Astronaut Edgar Mitchell with Paul N. Temple. Ervin Laszlo is founder of *The Club of Budapest* which integrates spirituality, science and the arts and *The Laszlo Institute of New Paradigm Research* which promotes the scientific emergence of cosmos and consciousness to advance humanity at this critical time on earth.

WHERE ARE SOULS WHEN THEY ARE NOT ON EARTH?

Souls who are not in a body remain at *home* in the spirit world which is said to be near to us but invisible to most humans. Think of this as living in *Soul City.* In your *spirit house,* there, are the special soul friends closest to you. When you reincarnate into an earth body, friends come with you. While on earth, each soul leaves a small essence or trace of their energy *at home* on the other side to greet friends who may return before others. Between incarnations, souls continue to learn and develop talents and new skills. Many odd occurrences can be attributed on earth to them such as manifesting specific fragrances of perfume or pipe tobacco smoke as *love messages* from deceased loved ones; leaving coins as surprise *hellos,* manipulating electrical lights and machinery to communicate as *a hug from beyond* and to make birds, feathers and butterflies appear, to mention a few. Some of your loved ones on the other sides may be learning how to communicate with you soon. Be receptive to signs of their communications.

DO BAD PEOPLE REINCARNATE?

When you die on earth, regardless of age or circumstance, it is a very sad time for humans. But at the right time, it is a joyful reunion for your soul to be met at *home* by loved ones in the spirit world. Think of this as returning home from a journey. Even the small essences of your loved ones still alive on earth are there for you, so you never really leave anyone behind. Each time your soul chooses to reincarnate, you make a plan with *Spiritual Elders* for your own spiritual and conscious evolution, but in a body on earth you have free will and that is when the plan can go astray. Free will can change a plan and have a negative consequence. After death and being welcomed *home* by loved ones in the spirit world, your soul is always learning and you review without judgment, the life just left behind. Some souls return home at a low energy level due to their free will, off-plan choices or bad deeds. They need intense *cosmic spiritual therapy* before returning to their soul friends there and the beneficial cycle of reincarnation. It is not easy being a human on earth. But it is important to have a comfort level with death because all human bodies die.

WHO BELIEVES IN REINCARNATION?

Several religions across the globe have variations of reincarnation in their beliefs. Some believe that we only, reincarnate as humans but others believe that we return as animals too. Over one billion Hindus and about five hundred million Buddhists including more than four million in the United States believe in reincarnation. The Dalai Lama is the spiritual leader of Buddhists around the world. But you do not need to be part of a religion to believe in reincarnation as it is a spiritual concept. Raising higher consciousness is a challenge, especially in these turbulent times in our world. More people every day are interested in reincarnation and being compassionate towards our earth, humans and all living beings.

WHO AM I? WHAT AM I DOING HERE?

Did you ever wonder: Who am I? What am I doing here? What is the meaning of life? There must be a reason why we are all here. Great thinkers and scientists such as Einstein recognized order and interconnections in the Universe. Asking why we are here on earth is an age old question for seekers.

Perhaps reincarnation is the answer. Doesn't it answer the question as to what else has meaning to our existence on earth? Science and Spirituality are converging in quantum physics everyday. This book is an introduction to reincarnation. It is to show that souls remember and recognize the *before love* from past lives in loved ones in their current lifetimes regardless of the nationality, colour of skin or gender, now… or then.

It seems the biggest life lessons throughout history are still… to overcome and accept religion, nationality, skin colour, gender and other differences of our fellow humans and that we are all connected as ONE. We are all part of the Divine Plan.

That is an on-going soul quest lesson that takes many lifetimes to learn.

Reincarnation and Famous People

You can research many people with connections to reincarnation. Here are a few to start.

Richard Gere, George Harrison, Carol Bowman, Sylvia Cranston, Eckhart Tolle, Louise Hay, Shirley MacLaine, Bob Olsen, Dr. Ian Stevenson, James Van Praagh, Patricia-Rochelle Diegel, Vicki Mackenzie, Doreen Virtue, Dr. Brian Weiss, Marianne Williamson, Yogananda

Famous People and Quotes on Reincarnation:

Elvis Presley studied at the Self-Realization Fellowship with Sri Daya Mata in Los Angeles. "Re-incarnation has gotta be real – it explains a lot about why people are the way they are." *Elvis Presley*

"You are not a human being in search of a spiritual experience. You are a spiritual being immersed in a human experience."

"We are one, after all, you and I. Together we suffer, together exist, and forever will recreate each other."

"Love is the affinity which links and draws together the elements of the world."

Pierre Teilhard De Chardin

"All the world's a stage,
And all the men and women merely players;
They have their exits and their entrances,
And one man in his time plays many parts."

— *William Shakespeare,* from As You Like It

"We are immortal souls in human frames." *-Alexander Pope*

"I believe ... that the soul of man is immortal and will be treated with justice in another life, respecting its conduct in this."

"I look upon death to be as necessary to the constitution as sleep. We shall rise refreshed in the morning." —*Benjamin Franklin*

"I know I am deathless. No doubt I have died myself ten thousand times before. I laugh at what you call dissolution, and I know the amplitude of time." —*Walt Whitman*

"I'm a great believer in the hereafter, in karma, in reincarnation. It does make sense. I believe that God is not just a law-giver, but a creative artist, the greatest of all. And what characterises artists is that they want to redo their work. Maybe it didn't come off perfectly, so they want to see it done again, and improved. Reincarnation is a way for God to improve his earlier works." —Norman Mailer

"We give thanks for places of simplicity and peace;
Let us find such a place within ourselves." -*Michael Leunig*

"So as through a glass and darkly, the age long strife I see, where I fought in many guises, many names, but always me." —*General George S. Patton*

"This life is only one of a series of lives which our incarnated part has lived. I have little doubt of our having pre-existed; and that also in the time of our pre-existence we were actively employed. So, therefore, I believe in our active employment in a future life, and I like the thought." —*General Charles Gordon*

"Why should we be startled by death? Life is a constant putting off of the mortal coil - coat, cuticle, flesh and bones, all old clothes." —*Henry David Thoreau*

"I am confident that there truly is such a thing as living again, that the living spring from the dead, and that the souls of the dead are in existence." —*Socrates*

"All pure and holy spirits live on in heavenly places, and in course of time they are again sent down to inhabit righteous bodies." —*Jewish historian Josephus*

"Souls are poured from one into another of different kinds of bodies of the world." —*Gnostic Gospels: Pistis Sophia*

"I am very sure, that my spirit will live on in a different place, as it has lived many times before. Yes, of course I believe in reincarnation! I know that in previous lives I've lived in France, and long before that in Egypt." -*Tina Turner*

"Important encounters are planned by the soul long before the bodies see each other" - *Paulo Coelho*

"The goal is not to be better than the other man, but your previous self" -*The Dalai Lama*

Glossary

Abolitionist- (Latin root: to annul, to put out of existence) NOUN-one who wants the end of anything; especially applied to slavery in the United States

Adopted- (Latin root: to choose) VERB- to take into one's own family

Coincidentally- (Latin root: to happen at same point of time and space) ADVERB

Compassionate- (Latin root: to suffer with another) ADJECTIVE- sympathy

Crooned- (Dutch root: imitative of sound) VERB- to sing in a low humming tone

Emancipation-(Latin root: to set free from servitude or slavery) NOUN- deliverance from bondage or controlling influence; liberation

Freedom Land- (Latin root: not under the rule of others) NOUN-place of liberty; exempt from slavery

Fugitive-(Latin root: to flee) ADJECTIVE- a running from danger or pursuit

Glory Land- (Latin: to celebrate) NOUN- a place of splendor and happiness

Psychiatrist- (Greek root: psych for soul; iatros for physician) NOUN- medical treatment of the mind by a trained doctor

Quaker- (Anglo-Saxon root: to quake or shake) NOUN- a religious sect with strong social justice beliefs; they were called The Society of Friends; one not hostile; one who looks with favour upon a cause; especially important during The Slave Trade from Africa to America; many Quakers became Abolitionists and in Britain, prominent Quakers were instrumental in changing laws to create Emancipation in The Slavery Abolitionist Act of 1834 for all of the British Empire including Canada in British North America.

Underground Railroad- (root: underground is secrecy; railroad is transporting of 'cargo' which were fugitive slaves) NOUN- it was not an actual steel railroad but secret routes to 'steal away' and transport black slaves from southern plantations by way of a network of safe houses, and hide-outs with a goal of reaching northern U.S. free states or freedom in Canada with the help of abolitionists, free blacks, Quakers, sympathizers and Indigenous people; thousands escaped to Canada, Mexico, Florida and elsewhere.

Bibliography

Bowman, Carol- Children's Past Lives: How Past Life Memories Affect Your Child. 1997. Bantam Books, New York

Cranston, Sylvia-Phoenix Fire Mystery: An East-West Dialogue on Death and Rebirth from the Worlds of Religion, Science, Psychology, Philosophy.1998. Theosophical University Press, Pasadena, California

Dwyer, Wayne; Garnes, Dee-Memories of Heaven: Children's Astounding Recollections of the Time Before They Came to Earth. 2015. Hay House Publishing, Carlsbad, California

Hay, Louise L. -You Can Heal Your Life. 1984. Hay House Publisher, Carlsbad, California

Laszlo, Ervin- The Intelligence of the Cosmos. 2018. Inner Traditions, Rochester, Vermont; Toronto, Canada

Leininger, Bruce and Andrea; with Ken Gross- Soul Survivor- The Reincarnation of a WWII Fighter Pilot. 2009. Hachette Books, Grand Central Publishing New York, N.Y.

Moody, Raymond A. Jr., M.D. and Perry, Paul- Coming Back: A Psychiatrist Explores Past-Life Journeys. 1990 Reprinted 2016. Sakkara Productions Publishing, Paradise, AZ.

Newton, Michael, Ph.D.- Memories of the Afterlife-Life – Between Lives: Stories of Personal Transformation. 2009. Llewellyn Publications, Woodbury, Minnesota

Nickelodeon Graphic Books and TV Series- Avatar: The Last Airbender

Nickelodeon Graphic Books and TV Series- Avatar: The Legend of Korra

Olson, Bob- Answers About The Afterlife- A Private Investigator's 15-Year Research Unlocks the Mysteries of Life after Death. 2014. Building Bridges Press, Kennebunkport, ME

Sadlier, Rosemary-The Kids Book of Black Canadian History- 2003. Kids Can Press, Toronto, Ontario

Shadd, Adrienne; Cooper, Afua; Smardz Frost, Karolyn- The Underground Railroad: Next Stop, Toronto! 2002. Natural Heritage Books, The Dundurn Group, Toronto, Ontario

Stevenson, Ian, M.D.-Twenty Cases of Suggestive Reincarnation. 1966 reprinted 1974. University Press of Virginia

Tucker, Jim B., M.D. (extension of Dr. Ian Stevenson's work) Return to Life: Extraordinary Cases of Children Who Remember Past Lives. 2013. St. Martin's Press, New York, N.Y.

Van Praagh, James- Adventures Of The Soul. 2014. Hay House Publications, Carlsbad, California

Van Praagh, James-Looking Beyond: A Teen's Guide to the Spiritual World. 2003. Fireside Book by Simon and Shuster Inc. New York, N.Y.

Van Praagh, James- Unfinished Business-What the Dead Can Teach Us About Life. 2009. Harper Collins Publishers. New York, N.Y.

Stearn, Jess-The Search for the Girl with the Blue Eyes.1968. Double Day & Company, Inc. N.Y.

Weiss, Brian L., M.D.-Many Lives, Many Masters. 1988. Simon & Shuster N.Y.

Weiss, Brian L., M.D.-Only Love Is Real- A Story of Soul Mates Reunited. 1996. Warner Books, Inc. New York, N.Y.

Books of Reincarnation

From the Bibliography page here are descriptive expansions for fascinating reading.

The Search for the Girl with the Blue Eyes

Author Jess Stearn researches the story of Joanne MacIver, an Orillia, Ontario teenager in recent time who accidentally enters into a past life as a young pioneer girl. Jess meets Joanne and the search begins for proof of her past life from one hundred years previous. It is spine tingling when they walk near her old homestead seeking her own grave as Susan (nee Ganier) Marrow who died in 1903.

Soul Survivor-The Reincarnation of a World War II Fighter Pilot

A young religious family living in the current southern United States have a life altering experience beginning when their young son frequently wakes up screaming that his WWII airplane is going down in flames. Author parents, Bruce and Andrea Leininger are to be commended for following through with tedious research that culminates with the dead fighter pilot, James Huston's widow confirming details that only her husband would have known in his lifetime. The WWII pilot reincarnated as a young boy and their combined experience expands our knowledge of spirituality and reincarnation.

Many Lives, Many Masters by Dr. Brian L. Weiss

How can a debilitating illness in a young woman culminate in a reincarnation experience that will expand human spirituality? This life altering first case study presents a professional dilemma and risk to a well-respected psychiatrist who becomes a world renowned past life regressionist.

Avatar: The Last Airbender

Although these are fiction stories created by Michael Danti Di Martino and Bryan Konietzko, these books, as high quality impressive graphic novels from the TV series are based on the cycle of reincarnation in training the hero.

Author's Notes

Thank you for reading this book. It covers immense times on earth and infinite time beyond earth in a few compressed pages. I was inspired to write a book to encouragement you to seek out more detailed information about reincarnation. I hope you consider this as a tiny cosmic gift to begin or to continue your spiritual growth.

I also honour the resilience of approximately twelve million Africans who were kidnapped, enslaved and were cruelly captured by slave traders of many different skin colors, religions and nationalities in the course of hundreds of years. Slaves were chained together in the filthy hulls of cargo ships to cross the perilous Atlantic Ocean. The ones who survived were sent to dozens of countries, colonies, states and Caribbean Islands and re-sold for profit but worked as free slave labor mostly in sugar cane, tobacco and cotton fields.

In reincarnation beliefs, those who were part of that blight in history whether black, brown or white skin at the time will incarnate in our current world to create some understanding of the wrong and make it right, not by revenge but by forgiveness, love and in honour of those millions of poor souls then.

The *Walk Free Global Index* estimates that today there are 30 million slaves on earth because of severe poverty or the unspeakable slave trafficking trade of women and children. It is shocking that there are still people involved in these inhumane atrocities. Let us use our newfound powers and knowledge to change the negative low energy vibration in the world to positive high vibration by helping in any small way we can.

Acknowledgements

My inspiration for creating this book came to me after I had a past-life experience into the American Civil War. Deaths then exceeded 750,000 which would be equivalent to over 7.5 million Americans today. It is comforting to hope that many of those souls are reincarnated now with the message that life is very precious and war anywhere on earth is avoidable and unacceptable.

High praise to all the brave authors, mediums, inspired and exceptionally special souls in the past sixty years who took the risks of writing about reincarnation experiences just when the world needs this information the most.

Thank you to my daughter, husband and family who encouraged my writing and to my son and daughter-in-law for keen conversation and to all of them for big hugs, love and laughter. Thanks to both of my kids for choosing me as your mother in this life. You and your families are my proud gift to the world and I feel that we all have traveled together many times with *before love.*

Thank you to my close loved ones for the lessons learned today and in many shared past lifetimes. I treasure our *soul learning* together in this cosmic high school called 'earth'. Thank you to everyone at Balboa Press and Hay House Publishing for giving me a media platform to share my accumulated thoughts, years of research and lessons learned.

About the Author

www.thebeforelovebook.com

Linda N. Thorn has had five decades of experience as an educator, therapist, author, free-lance writer and a keen interest in researching history, metaphysics, spirituality and reincarnation.

She lived in busy Toronto, Canada until an *other-worldly* after-death communication (ADC) from a long deceased loved one directed her to the natural beauty and soul calming waters north of the city. Linda is also grateful for a profound past-life experience into pre Civil War America. These two astonishing spiritual and paranormal connections, along with copious coincidences throughout the years have been her inspirational motivation to share this reincarnation introduction with readers of all ages from 9 to 99 years of age for the purpose of a more loving, peaceful and compassionate world of enlightened souls. She is also author of *Beautiful Joe- a true dog rescue story* www.thebeforelovebook.com

Printed in the United States
By Bookmasters